TURKISH
EMBROIDERY

TURKISH EMBROIDERY

PAULINE JOHNSTONE

VICTORIA & ALBERT MUSEUM

Published by the Victoria and Albert Museum, 1985

© Trustees of the Victoria and Albert Museum
Colour photography by Jeremy Whitacker
Designed by Tim Harvey
Printed by Van Leer, Holland

ISBN 0 948107 0 22

Turkish Embroidery

A French traveller to the islands of the eastern Mediterranean about the year 1700 said of the Greek women of Mykonos: 'Embroidery being an invention of the Levant they wear nothing without it, and to speak truth they excel even the French in that sort of work.'[1] He could just as well have made the same remark of Turkish women in the islands, or of the Turkish and Greek women of mainland Asia Minor, for everywhere around this area wonderfully fine embroideries have been made at least since the sixteenth century, and perhaps earlier. The scarves, towels and covers which Turkish families used in abundance in their daily lives in the seventeenth, eighteenth and nineteenth centuries survive in especially large numbers. Their graceful floral patterns were exquisitely embroidered on filmy backgrounds of natural linen and cotton in delicate colours offset with gold.

The Ottoman Turks came to Anatolia as marauding tribes spearheading the advance of militant Islam against the Byzantine Empire early in the fourteenth century. The fifteenth century saw these tribes progress from a series of aggressive frontier principalities to a great military nation, backed by sophisticated systems of law and administration, religion, social organisation and learning. By this time they were so far advanced in the practice of the decorative arts that they were making pottery and ceramic tiles of great beauty, and weaving sophisticated silks in emulation of the Italian silks which they imported. A further impetus was given to their silk industry when they finally captured Constantinople from the Byzantines in the middle of the fifteenth century, for this great city had been for nine hundred years the centre of the famed Byzantine silk production. Embroidery, the junior branch among the textile arts, must have played a part in Turkish life at least by this period (and possibly in primitive forms from much earlier), but we have little or no information about it, still less any existing pieces, before the middle years of the sixteenth century.

Very roughly, the embroideries which have come down to us can be thought of as 'heavy' or 'light'. Surviving pieces in the 'heavy' category, especially in the earlier centuries, are nearly all military accoutrements. Existing examples are relatively rare, and almost all come from booty captured during the Turkish expansionist wars which drove Turkish troops far into central Europe during the sixteenth and seventeenth centuries. The main items among these military artefacts are saddles and saddle cloths heavily embroidered in gold and silver thread, with smaller gold-embroidered pieces such as holsters and flask covers; coats with applied patterns of coloured leather; large tents or pavilions made of heavy linen with floral patterns in applied work; and military and naval banners.

Some of our best evidence for dating the earlier Turkish embroideries (that is those of the seventeenth century) comes from Hungary, which bore the brunt of the Turkish advance at this period. From their defeat of the Hungarians at Mohacs in 1526 until their final expulsion in 1699, the Turks occupied a large part of the Kingdom of Hungary,

---

1. Pitton de Tournefort, *A Voyage into the Levant*, Vol. I, p. 219, English translation 1718.

installing Turkish governors in the towns, and periodically conducting a more or less energetic guerilla war with the Hungarian population. The Hungarians greatly admired the handsome horse trappings captured from their opponents, and the aristocratic Hungarian commanders appear not only to have kept these items of Turkish booty for their own use, but also to have had copies made for themselves in Hungary, principally in Transylvania. It is now not always possible to tell which was Hungarian and which Turkish work. The horse trappings were embroidered in laid gold or silver threads in floral patterns which often recall the patterns on Turkish tiles and silks. At least one dated example exists: others can be securely dated to the seventeenth century by the occasion of their capture.[2]

The tents used by the Turkish army commanders in these same campaigns were made of heavy linen and decorated on the inner walls with applied shapes of linen, wool or even leather in the basic colours of red, blue, green and cream in the floral patterns which the Turks found so pleasing. Here again are simplified versions of the formally balanced compositions of tulips and carnations which are familiar to us from ceramic tiles and woven silks. The edges of the appliqué were turned under and hemmed down, and no further decoration in embroidery stitches or couched outlining was attempted. Like the saddle cloths, tents were taken from the Turkish armies in battle, but many were also imported into Europe, particularly into Poland where they were especially popular, through the Black Sea ports.[3] A later version of appliqué embroidery was popular in the nineteenth century. It was worked in felt rather than linen, and used for large hangings and prayer carpets. This type of work is also akin to Persian applied work in felt, which is frequently attributed to Resht on the Caspian.

Apart from military accessories, heavy metal thread embroidery was used in a religious connection for mosque hangings and prayer carpets. Every year the Sultan despatched a caravan, heavily defended against marauding desert Arabs, bearing treasure and a valuable cloth to the shrine at Mecca. The huge cloth, comparable to a tent, was worked with quotations from the Koran and used to cover the shrine (the Kaaba) during the period of the pilgrimage. After the year's ceremonies it would be cut up, and pieces distributed as holy relics to leading Islamic rulers and important officials.

Judging from existing examples religious pieces of this kind were more often embroidered in the eighteenth and nineteenth centuries, and it seems likely that the prized silks rather than embroidery would have been used for such purposes in the sixteenth and seventeenth centuries when silk manufacture was at its height.

Smaller items embroidered in gold thread on leather included wallets and document cases, which were also used as cases for the Koran, and by scholars for their books. Foreigners living in Turkish cities appear to have ordered small articles of this kind for their own use. Pieces embroidered with the owner's name and the date show that they were made throughout the seventeenth and eighteenth centuries.

The early years of the nineteenth century, during the reign of Sultan Mahmoud II,

2. See G. Palotay, *Les éléments turcs-ottomans des broderies hongroises*, 1940. A saddle cloth dated 1670, which is probably a copy of the Turkish style made in Transylvania, is shown at fig. 150. Fig. 149 shows a Turkish example from the Esterházy treasure, now in the Museum of Decorative Arts, Budapest. Another saddle cloth given by Bethlen Gabor, Prince of Transylvania, to Gustavus Adolphus of Sweden in 1626 is illustrated in A. Geijer, *Oriental Textiles in Sweden*, 1951, No. 104, pl. 44. Other notable collections of Turkish booty are that captured by the Markgraf Ludwig Wilhelm of Baden, fighting the Turks in eastern Europe in the 1680's, (Badisches Landesmuseum, Karlsruhe, *Die Türkenbeute*, 1970); and that of the Heeresgeschichtliches Museum, Vienna.

3. According to one Polish authority the imported 'oriental' tents were made in eastern Anatolia and were strongly influenced by Persian tent making, especially by the art of Tabriz in the reign of Shah Ismail (1501–1524). T. Mańkowski, *Polskie Tkaniny i Hafty XVI–XVIII Wieku*, 1954, p. 125.

saw a great change in Turkish dress, when the traditional long-skirted caftans were exchanged by the upper classes for the west European frock coat and trousers. As the century progressed the rising bourgeois and merchant classes all over the Turkish Empire adopted the immensely wide trousers and short waistcoats and jackets which previously had only been worn as outer garments by the lowest of the working classes. As these garments became respectable wear for the middle classes during the course of the century trousers and jackets were made as matching suits. The fashion for elaborate gold embroidery on jackets and waistcoats and on the pockets and seams of the trousers seems to have been started in the Turkish navy. According to one English commentator, the dress of the sailors and officers of the navy was among the most striking, being made of scarlet cloth richly worked with gold, but 'the abandonment of all these gorgeous costumes by the Ottomans dates from the time the state began to feel the weight of the immense expense they caused, at the beginning of the present century' (i.e. the nineteenth).[4] Gold embroidered suits of this kind were worn by civilians, possibly more in the provinces than in the capital, and by the courier (kavas), the traditional carrier of messages and organiser of travel (col. pl. 4.) On more sober garments gold thread was often replaced by elaborate patterns in couched braid.

All these gold embroideries, particularly the military equipment, the thickly padded work on hangings and Kaaba covers, and gold embroidery on suits and leather articles, would have been made by men, working in professional workrooms.

Gold embroideries of this heavy type are not very well represented in the Museum collection. The best of the military equipment, including saddle cloths, saddles and tents, is preserved in central European collections (see note 2). (The cover 354–1897, (col. pl. 3) which is worked in silver thread on red silk, can really be classed as 'light' work, but gives some idea in a more graceful style of the floral patterns on the saddle cloths.) A made-up piece in the collection consists of pieces of seventeenth and nineteenth century embroidery which have been joined to reconstruct a saddle cloth (258–1899, cat. 9). A small fragment of metal thread embroidery (Circ. 100–1933, cat. 10) may well have come from a seventeenth century horse trapping. There is no example of linen appliqué from a tent, but a nineteenth century felt appliqué prayer carpet is shown at cat. 18. Embroidered leather for clothing is represented by two identical pieces (T.292–1913 (cat. 12) and Circ. 624–1919) which may have come from a pair of sleeves or the front panels of a pair of boots.[5]

There are two examples of embroidered leather wallets made for foreigners. The larger (T.34–1918, cat. 13) carries the arms of the Duke of Newcastle and can therefore be dated to the middle of the eighteenth century. Although the embroidery is Turkish it was probably made up in England. A small wallet is inscribed on one side *Willm Whitman*, and on the other *Constantinop. An° 1676* (537–1872, cat. 14). A prayer carpet heavily embroidered in laid gold threads with some touches in coloured silks shows strong French influence in its pretty, flower-decked prayer niche. The eighteenth century saw a less warlike atmosphere in Turkey, and a growing interest in the manners of its erstwhile enemies. The French rococo style exactly suited this desire for the elegant life, and had a marked influence on Turkish decoration at this period (see col. pl. 8 and cat. 30.)

4. Fanny Janet Blunt, *The People of Turkey*, 1878, Vol. II, p. 53. Lady Blunt was the wife of a British Consul General in Turkey, and daughter of a British businessman and Consul. She had been brought up in Bursa and spent most of her life in Turkey.
5. A Turkish leather coat of the seventeenth century is illustrated in Géza Fehér, *Craftsmanship in Turkish-ruled Hungary*, 1975, Pl. III, etc.

Also in the collection is a portion of a Kaaba cloth for the year 1918 which is thought to have been made in Cairo (T.387–1960, cat. 16). It is worked with a quotation in Arabic script in highly padded gold embroidery on heavy black silk. It would seem that a great deal of heavy gold embroidery on large curtains and covers was made in Cairo in the later years of the nineteenth century and into the twentieth century.

Another type of small square cover which is represented in the Museum collection by four examples is thickly worked in gold but does not quite fall into the category of 'heavy' embroidery (cat. 15). The gold is less thickly padded and the background material lightweight. These covers are worked with regularly repeated floral motifs in metal thread on coloured silk grounds, and date to the late nineteenth or twentieth centuries, two hundred years later, that is, than the red and silver piece mentioned above. Many of them have come to light in the possession of Jewish families in Israel and Greece and information received from the owners indicates that they may have been made principally in Bursa.[6] Part of a seventeenth century cushion cover in the same style is illustrated by Geijer.[7] It seems likely that the pattern was originally developed for large covers on the divan, and later copied for use on the small squares.

Embroideries in the 'light' category exist in far greater quantities. The pieces that can be thought of as coming under this heading are worked in coloured silks on linen or fine cotton, with or without gold thread. The background materials are nearly always left in their natural unbleached state, although there are exceptions to this rule. Like the heavier metal thread embroideries, their patterns are almost invariably floral.

The Turks for the most part were Sunni Moslems, who interpreted very strictly the Koranic prohibition on the representation in decoration of the human figure and indeed all animate life, but unlike the Arabs, whose decorative art consisted almost entirely of intricate abstract linear pattern, the Turks relaxed the rule to allow the use of flowers. From the fifteenth century the painted tiles which so wonderfully enriched mosques and palaces, the ceramic bowls and plates, the luxurious woven silks, were all patterned with graceful yet formally arranged flower compositions. The most popular flowers, which were used again and again in the earlier years, were the rose, tulip, carnation, hyacinth, and sprays of fruit blossom. These flower patterns in ceramics and silks bear a strong resemblance to each other, and we have seen that many of the military embroideries were very close to them. Likewise the lighter embroideries in the earlier period are very much in the style of the silks. This flowery tradition persisted in the graceful towels, sashes and kerchiefs of later centuries. The range of flowers widens – sometimes to include fruits as well – and the patterns, which must often be adapted to the format of a border, become less formal, and frequently less well balanced.

Descriptions of the luxuriant gardens on the Bosphorus show that the Turks delighted in all flowers, real or silken. In Turkey as in other eastern countries certain flowers were sometimes endowed with symbolic meanings.[8] The chains of floral needle lace (oya) which decorated women's headdresses could be used as an expression of mood, or to show the wearer's situation, but it would be fanciful to try to read a message into every floral border on a towel.

Many of these embroideries must have been worked in people's homes, but there is evidence as early as 1628 to show that they were also the work of professional work-

6. I am indebted to Mrs. Esther Yuhasz of the Israel Museum, Jerusalem, and Mr. Nikos Hannan-Stavroulakis of the Jewish Museum in Athens for information regarding these small covers.
7. A. Geijer, *Oriental Textiles in Sweden*, 1951, No. 110, pl. 47.
8. Charles White, *Three Years in Constantinople*, 1845, Vol. I, pp. 307–8.

rooms. A description of the craft guilds of Istanbul in that year tells us that that of the handkerchief makers comprised one hundred men with sixty shops.[9] By the middle of the nineteenth century we learn from English residents in Turkey that professional workrooms were largely staffed by Greek, Armenian and Jewish women, because Moslem Turkish women were forbidden to work for commercial profit.[10]

Much fine and beautiful embroidery was made by Turkish women in the harem (that is the women's quarters in any household). Travellers to Turkey from the sixteenth century to our own time have remarked that it was an accomplishment which formed part of every girl's education: thus the Frenchman Nicolas de Nicolay, speaking of the Seraglio in 1550, mentioned two hundred girls '. . . et de dix en dix ont une matrone pour les instruire et gouverner et apprendre toutes sortes d'ouvrages à l'éguille.'[11] Early in the present century Lucy Garnett wrote, 'Needlework especially is held in great estimation, and for many years before marriage a girl finds occupation for her leisure hours in embroidering the sheets, towels, quilts, napkins and other articles which will later on figure in her trousseau and deck the bridal chamber.'[12]

Unfortunately, there is no way in which harem embroidery can be distinguished from work made commercially. It can only be said that types of embroidery which appear very frequently, or that have clearly recognisable patterns in unvaried techniques are more likely to have been made for the market. Harem embroidery was made for the use of the household, and therefore was more often a way of showing off a woman's best work and individual preference. It was also said, again speaking of the late nineteenth or early twentieth century, that some families, by bringing in all available aunts and cousins, virtually formed themselves into a workroom, and would sell their work to middlemen in spite of the religious prohibition.[13]

We do have a certain amount of information about the way in which embroideries were used. Their use for military purposes has already been mentioned. Apart from these heavy metal thread or appliqué pieces, numbers of large embroideries of a lighter type, which could be used either as hangings or as spreads for the divan, were worked in the sixteenth and seventeenth centuries and later. An ambassador to the Sultan in the 1550's tells us that when he was introduced to the presence the Sultan 'was seated on a rather low sofa, not more than a foot from the ground and spread with many costly coverlets and cushions embroidered with exquisite work.'[14]

The earliest of these large linen spreads were worked in a regular darning stitch in coloured silks on the counted threads of a fine loosely woven undyed linen. Many survive in part if not the whole, and almost without exception their patterns can be related to the patterns current in the woven silks of the period: in other words they were a cheap substitute for the very costly silks (cat. 1 and 2). (It must be remembered that however strange it may seem to our way of thinking, in the past it was the complicated process of silk production and weaving on a drawloom which required great expertise, and which resulted in an expensive and much sought after product. Hand embroidery could be produced by anybody with minimal capital outlay and no more skill than a

9. Evliya Effendi, *Narrative of Travels in Europe, Asia and Africa in the 17th Century*, translated from the Turkish by Ritter Joseph von Hammer, Vol. I, 1834, p.202.

10. Charles White, op. cit., Vol. II, p. 102. Bernhard Dietrich, *Kleinasiatische Stickereien*, 1911, pp. 5–6.

11. Nicolas de Nicolay du Dauphiné, Varlet du Chambre et géographe ordinaire du Roy, *Navigations et Pérégrinations . . .*, 1568, p. 67.

12. Lucy Garnett, *The Turkish People*, 1909, p. 269.

13. Dietrich, op. cit., p. 7.

14. *The Turkish Letters of Ogier Ghiselin de Busbecq*, trs. Edward Seymour Forster, 1927, p. 58. Busbecq's mission to Turkey as Ambassador from the Habsburg Emperor Ferdinand I was from 1554 to 1562.

certain manual dexterity.) This category of embroidery, by reason of the regularity of the stitching, combined with a lack of innovation in both design and technique, was almost certainly made professionally. Because of their very evident relationship to the silk designs, these embroideries are sometimes dated as early as the sixteenth century. It is possible that some of them were made as early as this, specifically those with well drawn designs directly comparable to sixteenth century silks. It seems likely that far more, if not most of them, were made in the seventeenth century. The fine, loosely woven linen on which they are worked appears to be the typical background material of embroideries from this area which are thought to date to the seventeenth century. Many designs are more like seventeenth than sixteenth century silks (for example cat. 2 and col. pl. 6), but above all very many of them are badly and carelessly drawn, with weak or fragmentary design, which seems to point to small workrooms with no professional designer (cat. 3 and 4). It seems unlikely that they would have been acceptable, even as substitutes, in a period when Turkish textile weaving skills had reached such a high standard of excellence. In addition to the large spreads, similar embroidery was also made for square covers and turban covers, and the type was continued into the eighteenth and nineteenth centuries.

Cushion covers for the divan in earlier centuries seem to have been supplied almost entirely by the silk trade. Very many velvet examples survive from the seventeenth and eighteenth centuries, and embroidered copies of these are sometimes found (cat. 23 and 24). They can be distinguished by their rectangular shape and the so-called 'lappet' patterns at each end, which are a constant feature of the velvets.

Julia Pardoe, an English girl who accompanied her father on a visit to Constantinople in 1836, was an infectiously enthusiastic writer on all things Turkish as she saw them. She describes the embroidered bedding in use in a well-to-do home as follows: 'At the lower end of each apartment are large closets for the reception of bedding. The slaves of the household no sooner ascertain that the visitor has risen than half a dozen of them commence removing every vestige of the couch, and depositing within the closet the mattrasses of embroidered satin, the sheet of gauze or worked muslin, the half dozen pillows of brocaded silk, and the wadded coverlets, rich with silver fringe, and gay with parti-coloured needlework, which have formed the bed.'[15] The French botanist Pitton de Tournefort, who visited Turkey in the earliest years of the eighteenth century and clearly encountered much less luxurious domestic conditions (as we can see from his description of a meal quoted below), also expressed his amazement at Turkish sleeping arrangements: 'The first time we were oblig'd to lodge among the Turks, we were puzzled sufficiently to know where we should lie . . . there was neither Bed, Couch, Bench, or Chair to be seen . . . when at once a Slave drew out of a Cup-board in the Wall, all the Materials for making our Beds.' He goes on to describe the bedding ('three Quilts, very scanty and very hard') but obviously in this household there was no embroidery.[16]

Embroidery came into its own for use at table and at the bath. Visitors to a house would be offered a spoonful of jam and a glass of water, perhaps coffee. Before this ceremony, a servant carrying a ewer and basin poured water over the guest's hands, and offered a fine towel, embroidered at both ends. (However, one English traveller tells us '. . . so does a lady lose caste for ever in a Turkish harem should she rub her hands with the napkin instead of passing it daintily over the tips of her fingers.')[17] A household of

15. Julia Pardoe, *The City of the Sultans and the Domestic Manners of the Turks in 1836*, 1838, Vol. I, p. 32.
16. Pitton de Tournefort, op. cit., Vol. II, pp. 79–80.
17. Mrs. Harvey, *Turkish Harems and Circassian Homes*, 1871, p. 61.

any standing owned quantities of these long fine towels (called *makrama* or *peşguir*) (col. pls 19–28). In the middle of the sixteenth century the Imperial Ambassador Ghiselin de Busbecq tells us that embroidered towels were even given as prizes in archery competitions.[18] Nearly two hundred years later it seems that they were still given for this purpose, albeit in rather different circumstances. Lady Mary Wortley Montague, visiting the Court in Vienna in 1716, found the Empress's ladies competing against each other in a shooting competition, aiming at three oval pictures (with guns, not bows). 'Near the Empress was a gilded trophy, wreathed with flowers, and made of little crooks, on which were hung rich Turkish handkerchiefs, tippets, ribbons, laces and etc. for the small prizes. . .'[19]

Several writers describe meals in Turkish houses. Tournefort, again, has left this description: 'When the hour of eating is come, they spread a piece of black Spanish leather upon the Ground or the Sofa, according to the number who are to eat. They who love Neatness lay it on a Table of Wood, half a foot high, upon which they set a great wooden Bowl with Plates of Rice and Meat. . . One Napkin of blue linen is handed round the Table, and serves all the Guests.'[20]

Other travellers speak of more elaborate arrangements. Ottaviano Bon, who was the Venetian *Bailo* at Constantinople (an office similar to that of Consul-General) from 1604 to 1607, just a hundred years before Tournefort's voyage, describes the meal served to the Pashas at the Public Divan, at which members of the public might lay complaints and petitions before the Grand Vizier. Here, after tables had been brought in, servants spread napkins over each person's knee, to preserve his garments.[21]

At least two travellers of the nineteenth century describe the 'tables' as circular metal trays brought into the room and placed on up-turned stools. The diners sat round the tray on the floor with embroidered napkins spread over their knees, and helped themselves from dishes which were placed on the tray. Julia Pardoe wrote of her experience in 1836 as follows: 'We had each possessed ourselves of a cushion and squatted down with our feet under us round the dinner tray, having on our laps linen napkins of about two yards in length richly fringed. . .'[22]

From these descriptions it seems that the practice in later centuries was to use metal trays as 'tables' for serving food, but travellers seldom mention table cloths, apart from the leather one described by Tournefort. Nevertheless it would seem that round cloths were sometimes used to cover the serving trays.[23] In the Museum collection there is a circular cloth of red silk (Circ. 740–1912, cat. 28), probably dating from the early eighteenth century, which could have been used as a 'table cloth' laid on the floor. It is embroidered in tambour work with finely shaded small trees and tents or pavilions, which perhaps indicate its use for summer meals in a kiosk or pleasure pavilion. Another cloth (Circ. 744–1912, cat. 30) is tambour embroidered on a similar red silk and also dates from the eighteenth century. It is square but has a large circular centre marked by the embroidered pattern. It too could have been used for the same purpose.

18. Busbecq, op. cit., p. 134: 'An embroidered towel such as we use for wiping our faces.' The word used in the original Latin (*Letters*, 1633 ed.) is *linteus*. A modern writer suggests that what was meant were the finely embroidered squares called *çevre*, which might better be translated 'handkerchief', (see p. 00). (Macide Gönül, *Some Turkish Embroideries* . . . in Kunst des Orients, VI, No. 1, 1969, p. 73.)
19. Lady Mary Wortley Montague, *Letters*, No. IX, published London 1763, Vol. I, p. 49.
20. Tournefort, op. cit., Vol. II, p. 79.
21. Report by Ottaviano Bon, quoted in N. M. Penzer, *The Harem*, ed. 1965, p. 105.
22. W. Turner, *Journal of a Tour in the Levant*, 1820, Vol. I, p. 56. Julia Pardoe, op. cit., Vol. I, p. 23.
23. Macide Gönül, op. cit., p. 75. Fanny Janet Blunt, op. cit., Vol. II, p. 32. A circular cloth of embroidered linen is illustrated in A. J. B. Wace, *Mediterranean and Near Eastern Embroideries in the Collection of Mrs. F. H. Cook*, 1935, pl. CXV.

A visit to the baths was a social occasion. Ladies visited the baths attended by a servant carrying everything they needed for a stay of several hours, which included innumerable towels. Julia Pardoe gives, as ever, a lively description of a day at the baths, and talking of the crowded rooms, mentions '. . . the busy slaves, passing and re-passing, naked from the waist upwards and with their arms folded upon their bosoms, balancing on their heads piles of fringed or embroidered napkins. . .' Then, 'when at length they (the ladies) venture into the outer hall . . . attentive slaves . . . pour essence upon their hair, which they twist loosely without attempting to dislodge the wet, and then cover with handsome headkerchiefs of embroidered muslin.'[24] Clearly the richly embroidered towels and kerchiefs were as much for display as for use.

Large towels with a looped cotton pile gave the description Turkish towelling to the English language. Since the purpose of the looped pile is to provide the greatest possible area of cotton to absorb moisture, it is clear that these towels were strictly for use, and there are many descriptions of the bathers wrapping themselves in large towels as they rested after a period in the hottest room. Nevertheless it is hard for us to imagine putting so much fine embroidery in silk and gold thread on a towel for drying oneself. The looped towels in the collection are all very large, and have deep borders of plain weave at each end to carry the embroidery (col. pl. 17). It has been said that the looped pile was only used on towels from the nineteenth century onwards,[25] but although this theory is supported by the type of embroidery found on existing examples there appears to be no proof that they were not made earlier.

For men there were barber robes of silk to wear as a protection during shaving. The neck openings of these circular robes were often very finely embroidered. The collection includes three silk robes and one seventeenth century example of fine linen, as well as a particularly beautiful neckpiece from a robe, tambour embroidered in soft pastel colours. (col. pls 9–11).

The embroideries which we describe loosely in English as towels are legion. They come in all sizes from the large bath towel (some 80 to 90 cm wide by 160 to 170 cm long), to the small rectangular towel or napkin, and with embroidery of every standard from the most remarkable virtuosity to the frankly botched. The best of them are worked on the finest linen or gossamer cotton, the coarsest on stiff, rough cotton, or hemp. Some of the background materials are decorated in the weave, either with groups of silk warp stripes at the edges of the loom width, or with horizontal weft stripes, perhaps in silk or in a coarser cotton thread. Obviously those (relatively few) embroideries which are actually worked on silk backgrounds are not those which are used as towels. The coloured embroidery threads are almost always silk, whether the finest floss or the coarsest quality made from broken cocoons and waste. (It must be remembered that Turkey and the European provinces of the Turkish empire produced a very large quantity of silk in the period we are considering.) The brilliant colours are often lavishly enriched with gold thread.

As we have seen, these long pieces were used as towels and napkins. Similar pieces could be used as scarves (see for example fig. i) and sashes, and when the strip of linen was very narrow, that is to say about 20 cm wide, they were used as drawstrings to thread through the tops of the wide trousers worn by men and women (cat. 62–64).

24. Julia Pardoe, op. cit., Vol. I, p. 133, and the same author in *Beauties of the Bosphorus*, 1861, p. 16. The quotation about wrapping the hair from this work appears to be a paraphrase from her description of her own visit to the baths in the *City of the Sultans*.

25. Burton Yost Berry, *Old Turkish Towels II*, in The Art Bulletin, Chicago, 1938, p. 254. Burton Berry found four dated towels of this type, all between 1820 and 1855.

Teptil. Grand seigneur incognito.

Figs. i–iii are reproduced from *Türkische Gewänder u.*
Osmanische Gesellschaft im 18. Jahrhundert
Facsimile reproductions from a collection of
watercolours of about 1760 in the German
Archaeological Institute, Istanbul ed. Klaus Tuchelt.
Graz, 1966, pls. 45, 201, and 204 respectively.

Fig. i Grand seigneur incognito. (The Grand Seigneur
was the Sultan. The embroidered scarf hides the
turban which would have indicated his rank.)

Many of these long narrow waistbands, called *uçkur*, had finely embroidered ends, and the collection also includes a number of them with coarser, 'peasant'-style embroidery. Women wore long sashes over their caftans or *entari*. In the middle of the sixteenth century Nicolay illustrates several women, including the Validé Sultan (the mother of the Sultan), wearing long narrow sashes, but all, as drawn by him, are not embroidered but decorated with stripes in the weave. Two of his illustrations show women in outdoor dress wearing long headscarves with an embroidered border on all four sides and fringes at the ends.[26] Existing long scarves and towels are embroidered at the ends only, and it is impossible to say now whether Nicolay's sketches are literally accurate, or whether he added a border for artistic effect.

The elegant girls painted by the Turkish artist Levni, court painter to Sultan Ahmed III in the first quarter of the eighteenth century, express in their diaphanous flowing garments the very spirit of these delicate embroideries. In particular a portrait of a girl sleeping shows a long embroidered scarf tucked behind her head which we could almost identify with the one illustrated in col. pl. 13.[27]

At this same period, to be precise in 1717, in the letter which includes the now famous description of her own Turkish dress, Lady Mary Wortley Montague, wife of the British Ambassador to the Ottoman court, suggests that for those who cannot afford diamonds, embroidery is the next best thing: 'Over this (my caftan) is the girdle, of about four fingers broad, which, all that can afford it, have entirely of diamonds or other precious stones; those, who will not be at that expence, have it of exquisite embroidery on sattin; but it must be fastened before with a clasp of diamonds.' And again, 'The headdress is composed of a cap. . . This is fixed on one side of the head, hanging a little way down with a gold tassel, and bound on, either with a circle of diamonds (as I have seen several) or a rich embroidered handkerchief.'[28]

A high-ranking lady of the Seraglio illustrated by Octavian Dalvimart at the turn of the eighteenth/nineteenth centuries wears a wide sash about her hips which also has a recognisable embroidered border.[29] Slightly later in the nineteenth century the fashion appears to have been for a large square sash, folded and draped to allow a point to fall at the back.[30]

As well as the long towels or scarves, many of these fine embroideries are made as squares. The traditional uses for embroidered squares were not as sashes but as covers or wrappers. In a house without drawers almost anything placed on shelves or in presses – folded clothes, bed linen etc. – was covered by a cloth or wrapper. Anything carried through the streets was so wrapped (fig. ii), any gift was wrapped, as well as letters, money, even wages. (Paper envelopes for letters were not introduced until the nineteenth century.)

The finest embroidered squares, called *çevre*, could be used as head coverings (as in Lady Mary's description above), as ceremonial handkerchiefs, or as wrappers for the Koran or other valued books, or indeed any valuable object or present. It appears to have been the practice of some of the sultans to walk among the concubines of the Seraglio and to indicate the chosen girl by throwing her a handkerchief.[31] It was probably such a

26. Nicolay, op. cit., illustrations following pp. 66, 68, 75. Later illustrations of Turkish women in outdoor dress invariably show veils of undecorated white muslin covering the head and face.

27. S. K. Yetkin, *L'ancienne peinture turque du XIIme au XVIIIme siècle*, 1970, pl. 9.

28. Lady Mary Wortley Montague, *Letters*, No. XXIX dated April 1717, published London 1763, Vol. II, p. 27.

29. *The Costume of Turkey* (after sketches by O. Dalvimart), printed for W. Miller, London 1804, fig. 60.

30. Thomas Allom and Robert Walsh, *Constantinople and the Scenery of the Seven Churches of Asia Minor*, n.d. (c.1839), illustration 'The Favourite Odalique', Vol. II between pp. 78–9.

Femmes Turques masquées allant au bain

Fig. ii Veiled lady going to the bath. Her attendant
carries her possessions wrapped in an embroidered
cover.

square that Busbecq meant when he described the prize given in archery competitions as 'linteus', although his translator has used the word towel (see p. 11 above). The Museum collection includes several square embroideries of varying dates which must come under this heading, among which are two very fine but unfortunately incomplete pieces worked on silk gauze (col. pl. 18 and cat. 46). These two pieces appear to be comparable in quality to a group of fine veils in Sweden which can be dated with reasonable accuracy from historical records to the second and third decades of the eighteenth century.[32] All are worked on fine silk, sometimes coloured and sometimes white or cream, and all have borders embroidered in coloured silks and gold with elaborate diagonal motifs in each corner. The designs have been strongly influenced by the spirit of west European rococo which, as we have already seen, was much in vogue in Turkey at this period, and this also applies to the graceful floral patterns of the two fragmentary veils under discussion. Neither of these is worked in gold thread but the embroidery in double running stitch is exceptionally fine.

Large square covers called *bohçe* were used for the wrapping of clothes and other objects of suitable size, and some of these, although worked on fine linen, are strengthened with a lining of coarser cotton finished on the back with a silk facing on all four sides (col. pl. 1). Very fine embroidery was often done on the covers used to protect the magnificently complicated turbans of the Ottoman Turks when they were not in use. A turban cover can usually be recognised by the small circle marked by the embroidered pattern in the centre of the square (col. pl. 16).

By the middle of the nineteenth century commercial workrooms were producing embroidered lengths of fine muslin or silk for women's trousers (*shalwar*), and shaped pieces for ladies' overdresses (*entari*) (cat. 67 and 68). From Charles White, an Englishman who lived in Turkey from 1842 to 1844, we learn that these workrooms were situated up and down the shores of the Bosphorus, and he also tells us that the embroideresses were Catholic, Armenian or Greek. It seems that they produced work for sale in the bazaars and perhaps for export as well. Charles White said of these embroideries that those decorated with the Sultan's *tughra*, or official monogram, and with mottoes or pious quotations, were always intended for sale to foreigners, who thought that the Islamic script lent an exotic touch to the work (col. pls 30 and 31). It is far from being the case that the *tughra* suggests an owner from the imperial Seraglio: on the contrary, according to White, Turkish ladies did not wear such things, except occasionally as sashes.[33] In practice the script was frequently mangled in the embroidery, so that it is seldom possible to read the inscriptions, which in any case appear to have been extremely hackneyed. Possibly this is precisely because the embroideresses were not Moslems.

By the end of the nineteenth century frequently repeated motifs were stamped on to the material with wood blocks, and these included the *tughra* and short mottoes, as well as the ever present floral motifs, many of them more European than Turkish in style.[34] By this time the export trade to Europe, especially to central Europe and Germany, had become very considerable. At the same time quality was declining disastrously, and for

31. N. M. Penzer, *The Harem*, ed. 1965, p. 181.
32. A. Geijer, *Oriental Textiles in Sweden*, 1951, p. 83, Cat. nos. 143–151, 153, 154. The piece Circ. 373–1929 (fig. 00) is closer in design to Geijer no. 162, which is attributed by her, probably mistakenly, to India.
33. Charles White, *Three Years in Constantinople*, 1845, Vol. II, pp. 102–3. This observation about the use of inscriptions for exotic effect on export work is also made by Bernhard Dietrich more than half a century later. (*Kleinasiatische Stickereien*, 1911, p. 48.)
34. Dietrich, op. cit., p. 35, figs. 8, 9.

Fig. iii Lady emerging from the bath.

this middlemen blamed the importers, who demanded ever more work for lower and lower prices.[35] It was at this time and in the early years of the twentieth century, that coloured background material, usually a thin cheap silk, began to be used for small light embroideries. (Good quality silk had always been used for some heavier work, and for very high class embroideries such as the Swedish group.) On such a material embroidery in cheap metal thread showed up to shoddy advantage. This thin gilt thread could be used on a chain stitch machine to reproduce a motif very speedily. Chain stitch or hand tambour work had after all a long and respectable history as one of the traditional stitches of Turkish embroidery, but whereas in the past it had been blended in innumerable shades of translucent colour, this expertise was now reduced by ferocious price cutting to hasty work which relied on the background material to supply some garish colour.

By the end of the nineteenth century most of the workrooms for the export trade appear to have been in Istanbul, a few of them employing as many as five hundred workers. The cottage industry was mostly in the coastal towns and villages round the shores of the Marmora. There were well-known 'family' workrooms in Izmid and Adabazar. Embroidery was not an industry at this period in towns where there was alternative employment for female labour, for example in Bursa (silk worm rearing and silk throwing etc.), and Ushak (carpet weaving).[36]

The Turkish contribution to the Great Exhibition of 1851 in London included quite a number of embroideries as well as many other textiles. The catalogue gives the names of a number of firms in Istanbul (Gulmezoglou, Horoussé, Floru, Marigo) and lists 'Muslin embroidered in silk and gold for ladies' shirts and dresses, embroidered by Gulmezoglou's daughter'. Mention is also made of embroidery by 'Hadji Ahmet's family', 'Hassan Aga's family', and so on, names which seem to show that it was not only Christian and Jewish women who embroidered commercially. (In fact the collection includes a towel which is, most unusually, signed by the worker, 'Ayeshe Hanim daughter of Hasan Aga' (cat. 51), but it did not reach the Museum through the Exhibition.) In making their report on the Turkish contribution the jurors said that they could not always make awards where these were due because so few names were given, but they did award a medal to 'Sofialioglou's daughter' for veils embroidered in gold and pearls with silk fringes.[37] Unfortunately it is now possible to identify only one piece from the Exhibition in the Museum collection (cat. 48). The only pieces which have been illustrated show a very strong European influence.[38]

Throughout the second half of the nineteenth century and later embroidery continued to be made for home use, while the workroom embroidery sold in the bazaars was not necessarily intended for foreigners. It is by no means possible to distinguish between the better workroom pieces and those made in the harem. A great deal of coarser but still well made embroidery was evidently worked in poorer homes for the family's own use. Fanny Blunt, who clearly did not share the admiration for embroidery shown by her countrywoman Lucy Garnett, describes a tradesman's house: 'His house is clean though very simple; his wife and daughters are ignorant and never taught a trade by which they might earn anything. Embroidery, indispensable in a number of useless articles that

35. ibid., pp. 23–4.
36. ibid., pp. 8–9, 12–13.
37. Great Exhibition of 1851, official catalogue part III, Turkey. Also Jury Reports, p. 484.
38. M. Digby Wyatt, *Industrial Arts of the 19th Century*, Vol. I, pl. X.
39. Fanny Janet Blunt, op. cit., Vol. I, p. 98.

serve to figure in the trousseau of every Turkish girl, and latterly coarse needle and crochet work, fill up part of the time. . .'[39]

The dating of Turkish embroidery, especially the pretty and colourful lightweight towels, scarves and covers which make up so much of the whole, is a difficult question indeed. It would seem that the most reliable information we have to date, particularly as regards earlier pieces, comes from western Europe. There is the evidence of the military pieces, as outlined in pages 5 and 6 above, there is the group of Turkish/rococo kerchiefs in Sweden (page 16), and there is also a certain amount of evidence regarding light embroideries, as well as military accessories, from Hungary.

All was not war in Hungary during the seventeenth century, and aristocratic houses made and used quantities of embroidered bed linen and above all table linen, as well as napkins or handkerchiefs which were given as gifts on all occasions, in much the same way as happened in Turkey. These were worked by family and maids, often under the direction of the lady of the house or a relative, but most sought after of all as embroideresses were Turkish women, whose ability in this field was greatly admired. There is a record in 1596 of a Hungarian nobleman writing to his wife from the battle front, announcing that he was sending home a Turkish woman from among the prisoners as an embroideress.[40] In another instance an aristocratic Hungarian lady corresponded regularly in 1611 with a highly placed Turkish lady, wife of the Turkish governor of one of the occupied towns, for the exchange of embroidery patterns.[41] Embassies to the Porte also brought back embroideries made in Turkey. Therefore in Hungarian collections there exist both Turkish pieces and Hungarian pieces influenced by or copied from Turkish patterns, whether worked by Turkish women or not. None of the obviously Turkish pieces actually carries a date, although it is thought by calligraphic experts that the inscription on one of them must date it to the seventeenth century. Some, however, were given by their owners to churches for use as chalice veils, and carry early eighteenth century Hungarian inscriptions added on the occasion of the gift. In these cases the embroidery is usually thought to be about thirty years older than the inscription, i.e. from the late seventeenth century.[42]

From these indications it can be deduced that certain types of pattern, especially on square veils, should be dated to the seventeenth century. A very typical pattern is that in which four large flower sprays spring from the corners of a square and between them fill the whole field (without a continuous border pattern). When this is allied to the background linen and embroidery colours thought to belong to the seventeenth century, it can fairly safely be assumed that the piece is in fact of seventeenth century date (col. pl. 15). The pattern appears to have continued into the eighteenth century, as for example in the cover T.33–1926 (col. pl. 16), where the bright pink of the flowers can probably not be ascribed to an earlier date.

Various theories on the chronology of styles, colours and stitches have been put forward,[43] but when they are examined closely it frequently turns out that they rest on subjective judgments and not on proven facts. This is not to say that they are not

40. G. Palotay, *Les éléments turcs-ottomans des broderies hongroises*, 1940, pp. 84–5.
41. ibid., p. 84.
42. ibid., p. 87 and figs. 9, 10, 11, 12.
43. Attempts at dating by these means have been made by Burton Yost Berry in his two articles *Old Turkish Towels* in The Art Bulletin of Chicago, 1932, and 1938; also by Macide Gönül, *Some Turkish Embroideries in the collection of the Topkapi Saray Museum in Istanbul*, in Kunst des Orients, VI no. 1, 1969, pp. 43–76. The articles by Burton Berry are probably by far the most reliable indications that we have for dating Turkish embroideries, but the points made do appear to rest entirely on his wide personal experience of the subject rather than on actual proof.

useful as guidelines, but it must be realised that they carry no proof in themselves. It is true that the colours in the embroideries we take to be the earliest, that is the darned hangings and covers made in emulation of silks, and therefore probably seventeenth or even occasionally sixteenth century, are very simple: usually red, blue, green and cream. It is a fairly safe assumption that more elaborate colour schemes are later in date. Some towels, which by virtue of the fineness of their working and of their linen background material are thought to be from the seventeenth century, have more delicate versions of these basic colours.

Statements that such colours as mauve and pale green first appear in the late eighteenth century may very well be true, but they do in fact rest on the assumption that the towels in which they appear are known to date to the late eighteenth century, which can by no means be proved. It can of course be stated definitely that any piece which includes aniline dyes cannot have been made before 1853, but aniline dyed threads do not in fact seem to appear in Turkish embroidery until well into the second half of the nineteenth century.

It has also been said that the outlining of motifs in a darker colour is a feature of eighteenth century work, but the embroideries on which this method is used very often give a strong impression of the nineteenth century.

The whole question is also bedevilled by the difference in quality between the best embroideries of the harem and the high-class commercial workroom, and peasant work. The earlier the finer is a rough but not necessarily an accurate guide. Again the rule of thumb statement that seventeenth century embroideries are worked on fine linen, eighteenth century on fine cotton, and nineteenth century on coarser versions of either, or mixed or striped weaves, is obviously true up to a point, but it once more assumes that there is some proof of the dating of towels worked on any of these materials.

A feature of gold and silver embroidery in Turkey, especially on the lighter pieces, is that the gold or silver thread was used with a needle like a silk thread, so that the embroidery could be worked in satin and stem stitches. This is not a method used very often elsewhere with metal threads. The more usual technique of laying the metal thread on the surface and couching it with a sewing thread is also used in some Turkish heavy embroideries from the seventeenth century onwards, but to a lesser extent. Another method of working metal threads, which is used on the leather pieces (cat. 12 to 14), is to lay the fine metal thread over padding on the surface, turning it on the outline of the motif, while at the same time crossing the back of the motif with a linen thread. The linen thread is brought to the surface to take a couching stitch in the angle of the metal thread each time this is turned.

The stitches used in the light embroideries are basically very simple. Their working requires great patience but no more skill than the counting of the threads of the ground material. The large darned hangings are simply worked in running stitches over an even number of threads (cat. 69). This was often arranged to produce a twill effect, but could also be used to cover the ground more closely by picking up a single thread at alternating intervals in successive lines of closely worked running, producing the same effect as a satin weave. Both these techniques fill in a pattern quickly with the minimum of trouble and were mainly used for large pieces.

Another technique used for large embroideries was laid and couched work in coloured silks (cat. 70). This type of work is finely executed on the cover 830–1902 (col. pl. 6), which can probably be dated to the seventeenth century because of its likeness to the silk patterns. Laid and couched work on heavy linen or cotton covers is generally much coarser and is almost certainly later in date. Possibly it was also made in the remoter districts of Anatolia, and some large pieces in this technique are Turcoman, or so-called Bokhara work. Basic techniques such as darning and laid and couched work continue through the centuries but can be seen to become coarser, using clumsier materials and more garish colours, as time goes on.

Very many embroideries, probably from the late seventeenth or early eighteenth centuries onwards, were worked in chain stitch. It seems likely that most of them were worked in a frame with a tambour hook, which is another quick method very suitable for use in professional workrooms. Some fine work in beautifully shaded coloured silks was done in this way, often on silk backgrounds (cat. 25 to 35).

By the second half of the nineteenth century chain stitch could be worked with a sewing machine, and this was used for cheap export work, with the result that quality deteriorated badly.

It is on the light domestic embroideries, also from the late seventeenth and early eighteenth centuries to the first half of the nineteenth, that the finest work is found. The outstanding feature of this beautiful embroidery is that both surfaces of the material were covered, so that the piece is completely reversible. Even so this effect was almost entirely achieved by the use of running stitches worked on counted threads in different directions. In order to create the reversible effect each line of stitching had to be worked over twice, or even in four stages, so that the regular spaces between the stitches in the original line were filled in (double running). The prettily shaded petals which are so typical of fine Turkish towels are achieved in this way with close lines of double running (cat. 73). More complicated versions are carried out with running stitches in steps or diagonals, which are also repeated to fill the spaces in the original line (cat. 71). Some of these stitches can be tightly pulled to draw the threads of the ground material together and create an openwork effect, which is also alike on both sides. A combination of steps and diagonals which requires four operations to cover the ground gives a result like fine but closely worked net (cat. 72). For brevity in the notes to the plates I have referred to these stitches, of which there are different versions, as compound double running.

Satin and stem stitches and French knots were used on the towels and light embroideries, and in later work some cross stitch. Gold thread, whether wire or flat strip, was used extensively as a sewing thread. (The lightweight ground materials were not suitable for couching metal threads.)[44]

44. Practical instructions for the stitches used in Turkish embroideries can be found in Macide Gönül, op. cit., where the Turkish names for the stitches are also given; and in Louisa Pesel, *Stitches from Eastern Embroideries*, 1913.

Short Bibliography

BERKER, Nurhayat — *Islemeler* (Embroidery). (Turkish and English). Istanbul, Topkapi Sarayi Müzesi, 1981.

BERRY, Burton Yost — *Old Turkish Towels* I & II, in The Art Bulletin, Chicago, Vol. XIV No. 4, 1932, pp. 344–358; and Vol. XX No. 3, 1938, pp. 251–265.

Turkish Embroidery, in Embroidery, June 1936, pp. 47–51.

CATALOGUE — *Turkish Folk Embroideries*. London, Museum of Mankind, 1981.

ÇELAL, Melek — *Türk Islemeleri* (Turkish Embroideries). (Turkish). Istanbul, 1939.

DIETRICH, Bernhard — *Kleinasiatische Stickereien*, Plauen, 1911.

GENTLES, Margaret — *Turkish and Greek Island Embroideries from the Burton Yost Berry Collection in the Art Institute of Chicago*. Chicago, 1964.

GÖNÜL, Macide — *Some Turkish Embroideries in the collection of the Topkapi Saray Museum in Istanbul*, in Kunst des Orients VI No. 1, 1969, pp. 43–76.

NEWBERRY, E. W. — *Turkish Towels and their Designs*, in Embroidery, June 1936, pp. 51–62.

PALOTAY, G. — *Turkish Embroidery*, in CIBA Review No. 102, Basle, Gesellschaft für Chemische Industrie, 1954, pp. 3662–3687.

WACE, A. J. B. — *Mediterranean and Near Eastern Embroideries from the Collection of Mrs. F. H. Cook*, London 1935.

Colour Plates

Plate 1. Cat. 5. Cover in darning stitch. 17th/18th century.

Plate 2. Cat. 6. Detail of a curtain or divan cover in darning stitch. 17th century.

Plate 3. Cat. 11. Cover embroidered in silver. 17th century.

Plate 4. Cat. 17. Gold embroidered suit. 19th century.

Plate 5. Cat. 18. Prayer carpet. Felt appliqué. 19th century.

Plate 6. Cat. 19. Detail of a cover. Laid and couched work. 17th century.

Plate 7. Cat. 21. Cover. Laid and couched work. 17th/18th century.

Plate 8. Cat. 27. Detail of cover or hanging. Tambour work. 18th century.

Plate 9. Cat. 33. Barber robe. Tambour work. 18th century.

Plate 10. Cat. 34. Detail from a barber robe. Tambour work. 18th century.

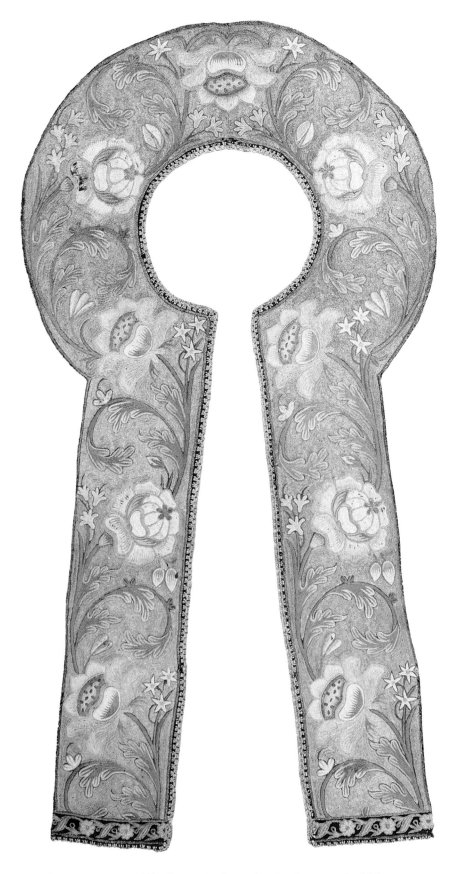

Plate 11. Cat. 35. Collar from a barber robe. Tambour work. 18th century.

Plate 12. Cat. 36. Border of a scarf or towel. 17th century.

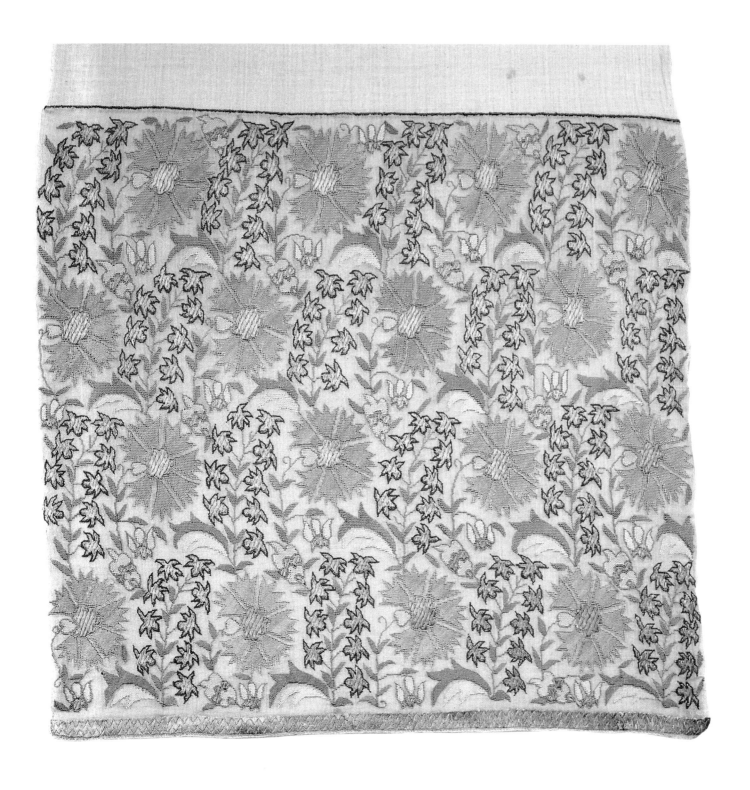

Plate 13. Cat. 37. Border of a scarf or towel. ? Late 17th century.

Plate 14. Cat. 38. Border of a scarf or towel. ? Late 17th century.

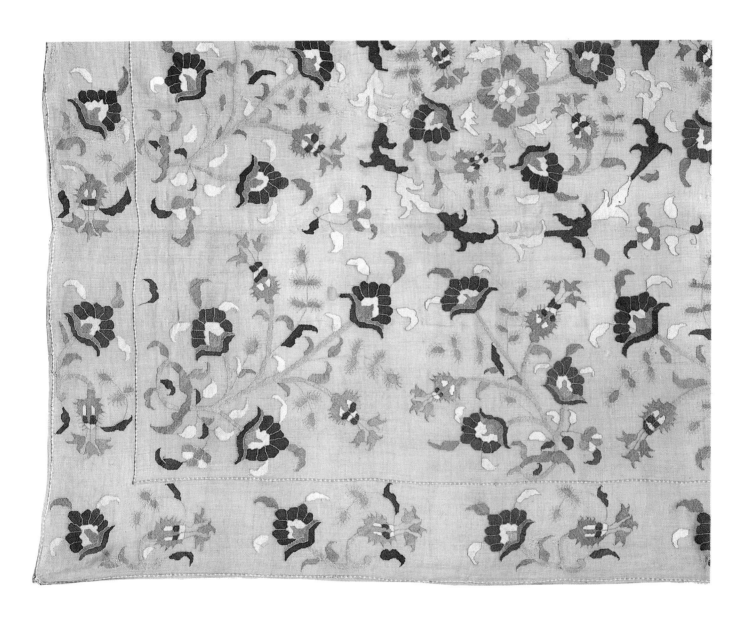

Plate 15. Cat. 42. Turban cover. Detail of one corner. 17th century.

Plate 16. Cat. 43. Turban cover. Detail of one corner. 18th century.

Plate 17. Cat. 47. Bath towel. Detail of one corner. 19th century.

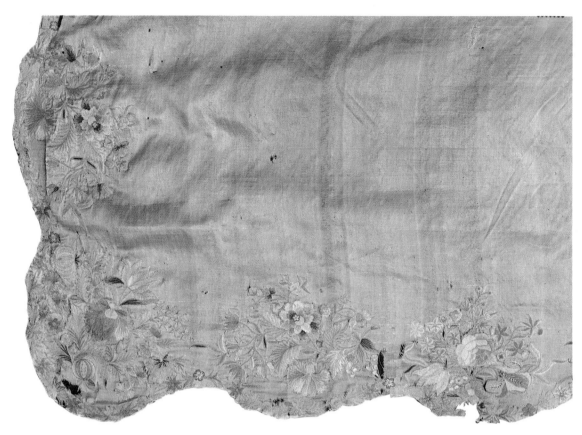

Plate 18. Cat. 45. Part of a square kerchief. Early 18th century.

Plate 19. Cat. 49. Border of a bath towel. 19th century.

Plate 20. Cat. 50. Border of a towel. 18th century.

Plate 21. Cat. 52. Border of a towel. 18th century.

Plate 22. Cat. 53. Border of a towel. 18th century.

Plate 23. Cat. 54. Border of a towel. 18th/early 19th century.

Plate 24. Cat. 55. Square cover. Detail of one corner. 18th/early 19th century.

Plate 25. Cat. 56. Border of a towel. Early 19th century.

Plate 26. Cat. 57. Border of a towel. 19th century.

Plate 27. Cat. 59. Border of a towel. 19th century.

Plate 28. Cat. 58. Detail of the border of a towel. 19th century.

Plate 29. Cat. 62. One end of a trouser sash. 19th century.

Plate 30. Cat. 65. End of a scarf. Third quarter 19th century.

Plate 31. Cat. 65. End of a scarf. Third quarter 19th century.

Catalogue †

†The pieces listed here are a small selection from the Museum's extensive holding of Turkish embroidery.

Darned Embroideries. Nos 1–6

The darned embroideries of the seventeenth century are worked in pattern darning in coloured silks on the counted threads of a fine linen background material. The darning is normally worked over three or four threads of the ground material and under one. The darning stitches are frequently stepped by one thread in each row to produce a twill effect (cat. 69). Parts of the pattern are left in reserve. The colours used are simple, and traditional for this type of embroidery: red, blue, green and cream, sometimes with a little black or yellow. The patterns conform to those found in sixteenth and seventeenth century Turkish silks, but are much less sophisticated in draughtsmanship. Sometimes indeed the drawing is extremely crude (cat. 4). The style was carried on into the eighteenth and nineteenth centuries, when both the background materials and the embroidery tended to become coarser.

1

1

Part of a curtain or divan cover.
Compare the design of the silk (cat. 7).
16th/17th century
240 × 144 cm
155–1893

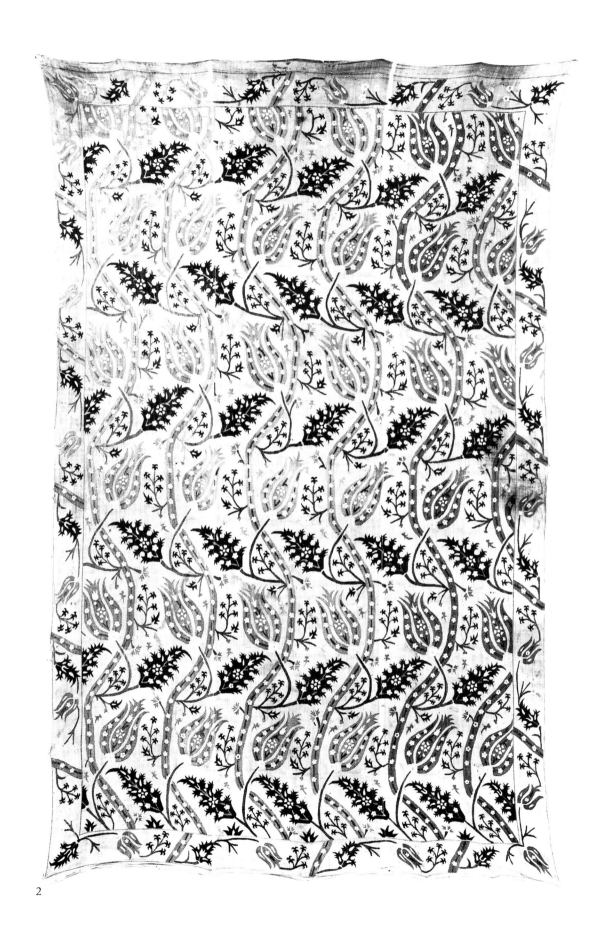

2

3

2
Curtain or divan cover. Compare the
design of the silk (cat. 8).
17th century
244 × 163 cm
121–1899

3
Fragment. Part of a width of a curtain
or divan cover.
17th century
121 × 58 cm
903–1892

4

7

4
Fragment. Part of a width of a curtain
or divan cover.
17th century
116 × 56 cm
(For detail to show stitch see cat. 69).
908–1892

5 COLOUR PLATE 1
Cover. Darning stitch on linen. This is
a typical silk design, more sophisticated
and better drawn than for example the
pieces shown in cat. 3 and 4.
17th/18th century
94 × 99 cm
888–1900

6 COLOUR PLATE 2
Part of a curtain or divan cover,
possibly a fine bed sheet. Darning
stitch on linen. The linen of this piece
is exceptionally fine and the darning is
taken in and out over single threads.
There is therefore no twill effect, as in
the previous pieces. The sinuous
pattern is a silk design of the type seen
in cat. 8, and also in the heavier
embroidered cover 830–1902 (cat. 19).
17th century
71.5 × 140 cm
T.99–1923

7
Woven silk. Part of a dress from a
royal tomb at Istanbul or Bursa. Twill
tissue. Red satin ground. 1/3 twill
binding for the pattern, in blue silk
and silver thread.
Turkish, 16th century
47 × 66 cm
741–1884

8

9

8

Woven silk. Part of a child's dress
from a royal tomb at Istanbul or Bursa.
Twill tissue. Red satin. 1/3 binding for
the pattern in silver gilt thread and
cream silk.
Turkish, 17th century
L. 75 cm
754–1884

9

Hanging or horse trapping.
Embroidered in silks and metal threads
on satin. Couching and satin stitch.
Quotations from the Koran are
inscribed in applied panels. Borders of
quilted satin. The bottom edge is
trimmed with a blue cotton fringe.
19th century (the centre panel 17th
century).
80 × 181.5 cm
258–1899

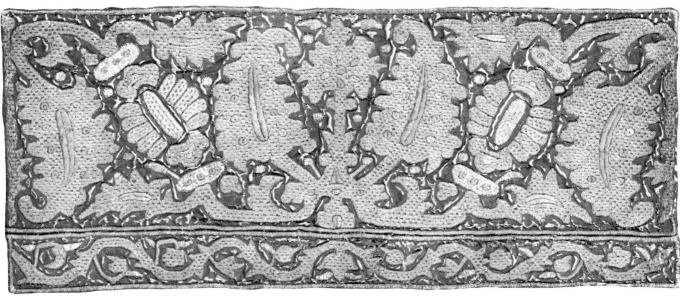

10

10
Fragment. Possibly part of a saddle cloth. Couched metal threads (silver and silver-gilt) worked over padding on a red satin ground. Details in green and blue silks in satin stitch.
17th century
21.5 × 53 cm
Circ. 100–1933

11 COLOUR PLATE 3
Cover. Red satin embroidered in couched silver and silver-gilt threads worked over padding. The large floral sprays springing from the four corners are typical of seventeenth century covers.
17th century
97 × 105 cm
354–1897

12
Fragment. Possibly a boot front (one of a pair). Black leather embroidered in silver and silver-gilt threads. The metal thread is laid on the surface and held on the back by a linen thread, which passes through the loops created in the metal thread each time it is turned at the edge of the pattern motif. This technique is also employed in T.34–1918 and 537–1872 (cat. 13 and 14).
17th/18th century
34.5 × 40 cm
T.292–1913
Given by Mr. A. Peters

12

13

14

13
Leather wallet or document case.
(back). Metal thread embroidery
worked over padding by the method
which is used in T.292–1913 (cat. 12).
The arms of the Duke of Newcastle are
worked on the back of the case in
metal thread and silks (see p. 6).
Mid-18th century
29.5 × 41 cm
T.34–1918
Given by Mr. Lionel Cust

14
Small wallet. Brown leather
embroidered in silver and silver-gilt
threads by the method which is used
in T.292–1913 (cat. 12). The front is
inscribed *Willm Whitman*, and the
back *Constantinop An° 1676*.
(see p. 6)
1676
11 × 19.5 cm
537–1872

15

16

15
Cover. Pale blue satin embroidered in
silver gilt thread, with a border of
dark blue satin. Couching and satin
stitch over padding. Similar covers
have come to light in the possession of
Jewish families, and are said to have
been worked in Bursa. (see p. 8).
19th century
74 × 73 cm
1058–1900

16
Portion of the border of the covering
of the Kaaba in Mecca, sent from
Cairo every year at the time of the Haj
or pilgrimage. The quotation from the
Koran is embroidered in heavily
padded silver gilt thread on black silk.
1918
29 × 98 cm
T.387–1960
Given by Lady Simpson Baikie and her
daughter Mrs. Morley Kennedey

17 COLOUR PLATE 4
Man's suit of red face cloth heavily
embroidered with couched silver
thread (silver strip wound on a silk
core). The suit comprises wide
trousers with leggings attached; a
sleeved waistcoat; over-jacket with
open hanging sleeves; a dark blue
embroidered fez (not shown); and a
striped cotton sash. Wooden buttons
covered in silver thread complete the
two jackets. This suit is reported to
have been brought back from the
Crimean War by a member of the
donor's family. It is probably the
uniform of a *kavaş* (courier). Turkish
naval dress of the early 19th century
was also said to be heavily embroidered
with metal thread. (see p. 7). By the
time of the Crimean War the Turkish
army was dressed in the west
European fashion.
19th century
T.25 to C–1964
Given by Mr. H. R. Robinson

18 COLOUR PLATE 5
Prayer carpet. Applied work in felt
outlined with couched silk and metal
threads. The fringe is a later addition.
Felt appliqué work of this type is
allied to the traditional linen appliqué
used in the decoration of military tents
in the seventeenth century. (See p. 6).
19th century
172 × 122 cm
T.85–1926
Given by HM Queen Mary

19 COLOUR PLATE 6
Large cover (detail). Laid and couched
work in coloured silks on blue silk,
with outlining in couched silk cord.
The repeating pattern of tulips and
carnations on sinuous stems compares
to silk designs of the period (see 619–
1893, cat. 20). The piece has been
extensively repaired.
17th century
148 × 178 cm
830–1902

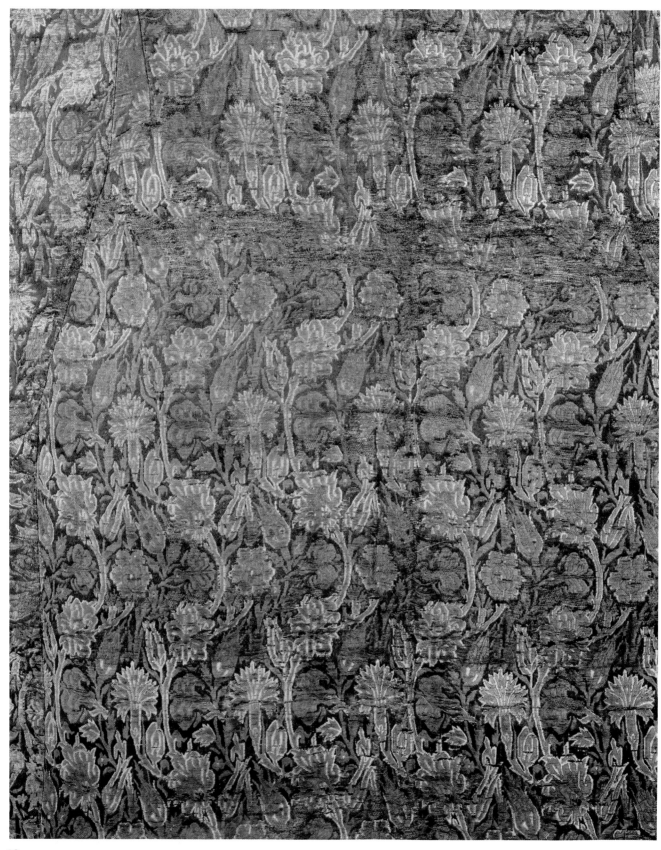

20

22

20
Woven silk. Red satin brocaded in coloured silks. Yellow, pale green and cream.
Turkish, 17th century
140 × 118 cm
619–1893

21 COLOUR PLATE 7
Cover. Laid and couched work in coloured silks and some metal thread on a red satin background material. Outlining in couched metal thread, now worn to the silk core.
17th–18th century
92 × 100 cm
T.733–1950
Given by Professor R. M. Dawkins.
(For detail to show stitch see cat. 70).

22
Fragment, probably the centre of a larger cover. Laid and couched work in coloured silks on a gold satin background material. Outlining in couched silk cord.
Late 17th century
48 × 44 cm
594–1894

23

Cushion cover for a sofa. Laid and
couched work in cream and blue silk
on a red silk background material.
Parts of the pattern are left in reserve.
Compare the woven velvet 17th
century cushion cover 423–1889
(cat. 24).
? 19th century
90 × 47 cm
934–1897

24

Detail from a woven silk cushion
cover. Crimson velvet with voided
satin ground brocaded with gilt and
silver-gilt threads.
17th century
134.5 × 66 cm
423–1889

23

24

25

25
Detail from a cover. Tambour
embroidery in coloured silks and
metal thread on gold-coloured silk.
Both embroidery and background are
faded. The pattern of tents and trees
compares to T.126–1924 (cat. 32).
18th century
65 × 122.5 cm
Circ. 745–1912
Given by Miss E. S. Baxter on behalf
of Miss Kate Baxter

26

26
Detail from a cover. Tambour work in coloured silks on linen. The pattern of four large sprays filling the four corners of this piece derives from the seventeenth century (see col. pls 15 and 16) but the coarse working and the shades of green and yellow used in the embroidery suggest a later date.
19th century
93 cm square approximately
905–1892

27 COLOUR PLATE 8
Detail from a large cover or hanging. Tambour embroidery in coloured silks on light green silk. The floral pattern in a rococo style trellis shows strong west European influence, as do the vases or 'shells' holding larger flowers in the corners. There is a medallion of these large flowers and leaf scrolls in the centre of the piece.
18th century
Whole cover 236 × 192 cm
434–1884

28

28
Circular cloth. (Possibly a table cloth, see p. 11). Red silk lined with cotton. Tambour embroidery in coloured silks. Some of the motifs show rococo influence.

Early 18th century
158 cm diameter
Circ. 740–1912
Given by Miss E. S. Baxter on behalf of Miss Kate Baxter

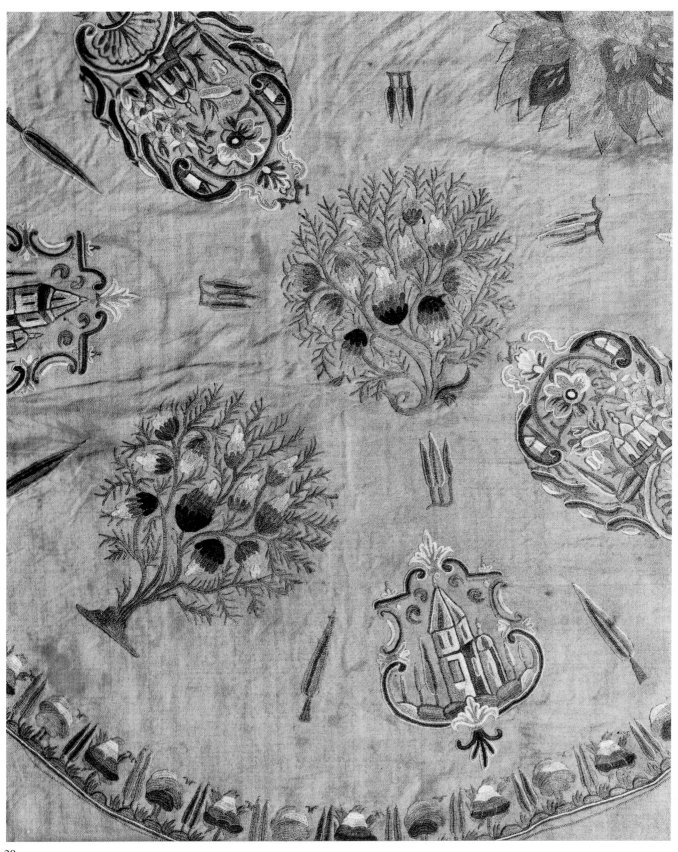

29
Detail from cat. 28.

30

30
Square cover. (Possibly a table cloth,
see p. 11). Dark red silk lined with
cotton. Tambour embroidered in
coloured silks and metal thread. The
motifs show strong west European
rococo influence. Detached needle-
made edging in metal thread. The

tambour work is very accomplished
both in this piece and in its companion
Circ. 740–1912 (cat. 28).
Early 18th century
116 × 112 cm
Circ. 744–1912
Given by Miss E. S. Baxter on behalf
of Miss Kate Baxter

31

Detail from cat. 30.

32

Cover. Tambour embroidery in
coloured silks on a faded red silk
background. Some metal (silver) strip
worked over thread padding, now
largely worn. The entire background
of the centre roundel appears to have
been worked in this way but now only
the padding remains, apart from faint
traces of metal thread. Pattern of tents
and trees with a sun in the centre.
(See also the cover Circ. 745–1912,
cat. 25).
18th century
128 cm sq
T.126–1924
Given by HRH the Princess Louise,
Duchess of Argyll

33 COLOUR PLATE 9
Barber robe. Tambour embroidery in
coloured silks and metal thread on
pale blue silk. There is a needle-made
edging of metal thread round the neck
opening. The embroidery colours are
badly faded, especially the reds.
18th century
169.5 × 96 cm
T.258–1934
Given by Mrs. Muriel Thomson

34 COLOUR PLATE 10
Detail from a barber robe. Tambour
embroidery in coloured silks and
metal thread on light green silk. The
design of a vase of flowers, which is
repeated to make a border round the
edge of the robe, is strongly influenced
by the French rococo style.
18th century
Whole robe, 138 × 51.5 cm
Detail, 20 × 13.5 cm
T.782–1919

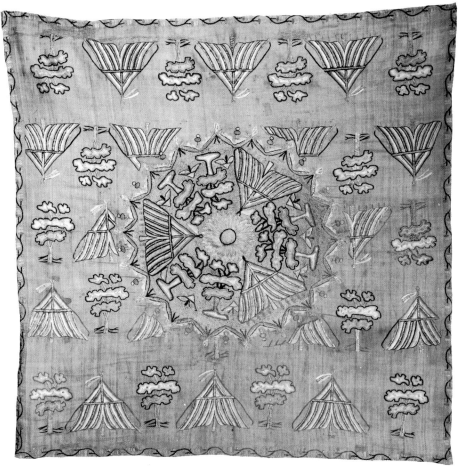

32

35 COLOUR PLATE 11
Collar from a barber robe. Fine
tambour embroidery in coloured silks
and silver thread on red silk. The
inside neck is finished with a needle-
made edging in silk. The embroidery
of the flowers, in this piece and in
other high quality tambour work, is
shaded in the same way as the typical
Turkish shaded double running stitch.
(Cat. 73)
18th century
L. 72 cm
601–1897

Compound Stitches. Nos. 36–41

The techniques which were used to
ensure that both faces of an embroidery
looked exactly alike seem to have
emerged at the end of the seventeenth
century and continued through the
eighteenth to the early nineteenth. It
could be said that the only stitch used
was a regular running stitch worked on
the counted threads of the ground
material, but a line of this simple stitch
could be worked over twice (double
running); or worked alternately hori-
zontally and vertically (double running
in steps); or worked over four times
in all by the addition of diagonal
stitches, which I have called compound
double running. Louisa Pesel simply
called the method double running in
steps and diagonals. The stitch is
described by her and by Macide Gönül
(see bibliography), who gives it the
Turkish name *muşabak*. It appears in

several versions. By the eighteenth century double running was worked in close lines of finely shaded colour (cat. 73). Another compound stitch also emerged consisting of a form of double running in steps which drew the threads of the ground material into an open net (pulled work, called by Macide Gönül *mürver*) (cat. 72).

36 COLOUR PLATE 12
Border of a scarf or towel. Embroidered in coloured silks on fine linen. Compound double running stitch. The unshaded colours (red, blue, green, cream and white) are similar to those of the darned curtains (cat. 1–4).
17th century
278 × 49.5 cm
Depth of border 72.5 cm
554–1899

37 COLOUR PLATE 13
Border of a scarf or towel. Embroidered in coloured silks and metal thread on fine linen. Double running and compound double running stitches. The style and colouring of this piece and 43–1879 (col. pl. 14) are very similar. They illustrate a recognisable group of embroideries which must have come from one centre or even one workroom.
? Late 17th century
W. 49 cm
Depth of border 44.5 cm
(For detail to show stitch see cat. 71)
T.171–1975
Given by Dame Joan Evans

39

38 COLOUR PLATE 14
Border of a scarf or towel. Embroidered in coloured silks and metal thread on fine linen. Double running and compound double running stitches. See also T.171–1915 (col. pl. 13).
? Late 17th century
75 × 46 cm
43–1879

39
Detail from a large cover or curtain. Embroidered in coloured silks on three widths of fine linen. Soumak stitch with some stem stitch. Red, blue green, yellow and cream. The large curving sprays are a typical seventeenth century pattern, see col. pls 7 and 15. The unshaded colours are also very usual in this period.
17th century
236 × 147 cm
T.52–1940
Given by Mr. Frank Brangwyn RA

40

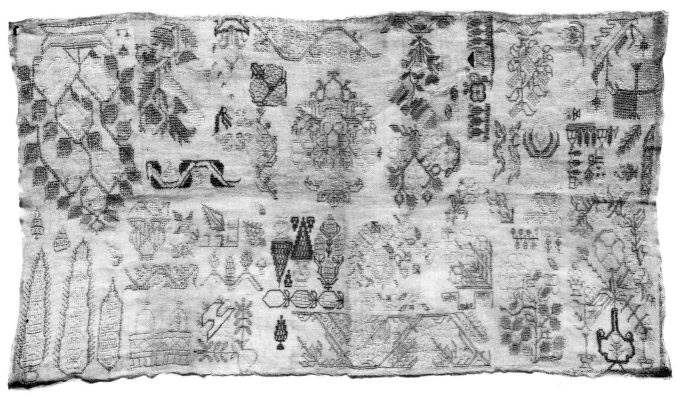

41

40

Detail from a cover or turban cover.
Embroidered in coloured silks and
some metal thread (now worn to the
silk core) on very fine linen. Double
running and compound double
running stitches. The colours (shades
of pink, blue, buff and green) are akin
to the scarves at col. pls 13 and 14.
? Late 17th century
116 cm sq
T.43–1940
Given by Mr. Frank Brangwyn RA

41

Sampler. Fragment of fine linen
embroidered in coloured silks with
random motifs. This sampler uses
many of the compound stitches of
Turkish embroidery: double running
in steps and squares, double running
in steps and diagonals, a pulled openwork ground, basket stitch, tent
stitch. Shades of red, blue, green and
cream, badly faded.
Early 19th century
26 × 48 cm.
T.325–1921
Given by Mr. G. D. Hornblower

44

42 COLOUR PLATE 15
Turban cover. Detail, one corner.
Embroidered in coloured silks on fine
linen. Compound double running,
outlining in double running, and satin
stitch.
17th century
110 × 114 cm
Circ. 145–1929
Given by Mr. Frank W. Taylor

43 COLOUR PLATE 16
Turban cover. Embroidered in
coloured silks and metal thread on fine
linen. Double running, outlining in
double running and satin stitches. The
pattern of large sprays springing from
the corners is typical of seventeenth
century embroideries, while the fruit
blossom and the leaf sprigs surrounding
the centre circle are both motifs which
occur in seventeenth century silks. The
colouring, however, must date this
fine piece to the eighteenth century.
18th century
123 × 119 cm
Loom width of linen 70 cm
T.33–1926
Given by HM Queen Mary

44
Turban cover. Detail, one corner.
Embroidered in coloured silks and
metal thread on loosely woven linen
joined down the centre. Double
running on counted threads in white,
pink and green. The motifs outlined in
stem stitch in brown, with whipped
running. Satin stitch border.
19th century
106 × 108 cm
Circ. 428–1930
Given by Mrs. C. J. Longman

46

45 COLOUR PLATE 18
Part of a square kerchief (çevre). Detail
showing embroidered motif from the
border. Exceptionally fine double
running in coloured silks on silk
gauze. The edge has been cut away
close to the embroidery and finished
with buttonhole stitch, presumably as
a repair, and two sides of the square
are missing. This piece and the
fragment illustrated at cat. 46
demonstrate the quality of the fine
kerchiefs mentioned by eighteenth
century writers (see p. 14). The floral
design of both pieces has been strongly
influenced by the French rococo style,
which is realised in a more
accomplished manner here than in the
fragment.
Early 18th century
74 × 78 cm
Circ. 373–1929
Given by Lady Battersea

46
Fragment. Part of a fine kerchief.
Double running stitch in coloured silk
on silk gauze. Shades of red and pink,
plum red, yellow, cream, green and
blue. (See also the remarks on Circ.
373–1929 (Colour plate 18).
18th century
W. 89 cm
946–1897
Given by M. Fulgence

47 COLOUR PLATE 17
Bath towel (detail). The main part of
the towel is woven with a looped
cotton pile, which gave the name
'Turkish towelling' to the English
language. The border embroidered in
coloured silks and metal threads in
double running and satin stitches.
19th century
169 × 91.5 cm
Depth of border 25 cm
45–1879

48
Bath towel (detail, one corner). Linen,
the main part of the towel woven with
a looped pile. Embroidered in coloured
silks and metal threads in double
running and satin stitches. This piece
can definitely be identified as having
come from the Turkish contribution to
the London Great Exhibition of 1851
but it is not possible to relate it to a
catalogue entry. (See p. 18).
Mid-19th century
162 × 91 cm
Depth of border 25 cm
757–1852

49 COLOUR PLATE 19
Bath towel (detail, one border). Linen
and cotton, the main part of the towel
woven with a looped pile. Embroidered
in coloured silks and metal threads in
double running, compound double
running and satin stitches. The design
is probably intended to represent the
Bosphorus.
19th century
177 × 73 cm
Depth of border 21.5 cm
T.509–1950
Given by Professor R. M. Dawkins

47

48

50 COLOUR PLATE 20
Fragment (border of a towel). Fine
linen embroidered in coloured silks in
double running stitch, with metal
threads. Shades of red and pink,
yellow, dark green and blue. Detached
needle-made border of metal thread.
18th century
60.5 × 20.5 cm
Depth of border 17.5 cm
T.261A-1934
Given by Mrs. Muriel Thomson

51
Border of a towel. Embroidered in silk
and metal threads on cotton. Double
running and satin stitches and pulled
work. Inscribed 'Glory to God. Ayeshe
Hanim daughter of Hasan Aga at
Bebek'. (Bebek is on the Bosphorus).
'Hassan Aga's family' is mentioned in
the catalogue as having contributed
embroideries to the Great Exhibition of
1851 (see p. 18), but this piece did not
come to the Museum from that source.
Mid-19th century
W. 73 cm
Depth of border 16.5 cm
T.103–1934
Given by Major Lee

52 COLOUR PLATE 21
Border of a towel. Embroidered in
coloured silks on fine linen. Double
running with some stem stitch. The
edge finished with buttonholing in
silver thread.
18th century
109 × 49.5 cm
Depth of border 12 cm
Circ. 196–1931
(For detail to show stitch see cat. 73)

53 COLOUR PLATE 22
Border of a towel. Embroidered in
coloured silks and metal thread.
Double running and satin stitch. The
edge finished with buttonholing in
silver thread.
18th century
135 × 50 cm
Depth of border 14.5 cm
Circ. 748–1912
Given by Miss E. S. Baxter on behalf
of Miss Kate Baxter

54 COLOUR PLATE 23
Border of a towel. Embroidered in
coloured silks and metal threads on
cotton. Double running, satin and tent
stitches. Detached needle-made border
in metal thread.
18th–early 19th century
132.5 × 52 cm
Depth of border 14 cm
T.458–1950
Given by Professor R. M. Dawkins

55 COLOUR PLATE 24
Square cover (detail of corner).
Embroidered in coloured silks and
silver-gilt strip on cotton. Double
running, satin stitch and pulled work.
Looped edging in silver-gilt thread.
The arcaded design shows west
European influence.
18th–early 19th century
100 cm sq
Circ. 197–1931

56 COLOUR PLATE 25
Border of a towel. Embroidered in
coloured silks and metal threads on
cotton. Double running with satin
stitch and some pulled work. Shades
of red, blue, green, orange and buff.
Early 19th century
244.5 × 35 cm
Depth of border 30 cm
T.460–1950
Given by Professor R. M. Dawkins

57 COLOUR PLATE 26
Border of a towel. Embroidered in
coloured silks and metal threads on
linen. Compound double running, tent
stitch and pulled work.
19th century
82.5 × 47 cm
Depth of border 12 cm
Circ. 740–1923
Given by Mr. Lionel Harris

58 COLOUR PLATE 28
Towel (detail from the border).
Embroidered in coloured silks and
metal thread on fine cotton. Double
running and compound double
running stitches and pulled work.
19th century
113 × 56 cm
Motif 15.5 × 8.5 cm
Circ. 742–1923
Given by Mr. Lionel Harris

59 COLOUR PLATE 27
Border of a towel. Embroidered in
coloured silks and metal thread on
linen. Double running and satin
stitch. Cross stitch edging with warp
fringe.
19th century
104 × 50 cm
Depth of border 17 cm
Circ. 631–1923

60
Border of a towel. Embroidered in
white silk on linen, with fringed ends.
Drawn thread work, pulled work,
double running with step stitch, and
tent stitch. Many towels of this type
have been found in Mytilini.
19th century
150 cm (without fringe) × 39.5 cm
Depth of border 24 cm
4189–1856

51

60

61

61
Border of a towel. Embroidered in
white silk on linen. Pulled work, satin
stitch and double running. The end
trimmed with a border of bobbin lace.
19th century
200 × 45 cm
4179–1856

One end of a trouser sash.
Embroidered in coloured silks and
metal thread on linen. Double
running and satin stitches.
19th century
287 × 24.5 cm
Depth of border 27 cm
T.254–1922
Given by Mrs. M. B. Walker in
memory of Dr. R. P. Cockin

63
One end of a trouser sash. Embroidered
in silver-gilt thread on linen. Double
running, worked on the counted
threads to give diaper patterns, satin
and stem stitches. Detached needle-
made border.
19th century
179 × 26.5 cm
Depth of border 26 cm
Circ. 6–1936

63

64
One end of a trouser sash. Embroidered in coloured silks and metal threads on linen. Double running, compound double running and woven hem stitching. Red, green, citrus yellow and beige.
19th century
221 × 22.5 cm
Depth of border 26 cm
T.209–1912
Given by Miss E. S. Baxter on behalf of Miss Kate Baxter

65 COLOUR PLATES 30 and 31
Two scarf ends. Embroidered in coloured silks and silver-gilt thread on cotton organdie, finished with a fringe of metal thread. Satin stitch. This is professional work, probably for the export or tourist market. The floral design shows strong west European influence. The sultan's *tughra* or monogram shown on both scarves has been simplified and distorted in the embroidery, but appears to be that of Sultan Abdul-Aziz, who reigned from 1861 to 1876. This dating would accord with the style of the embroidery. (See p. 16).
Third quarter 19th century
236 × 52.5 cm
T.25–1927
246.5 × 52.5 cm
T.237–1959
Both given by HM Queen Mary

66
Small cover. Embroidered in silver thread on pink silk woven with a warp stripe. Satin stitch and double running. Professional work for the export market.
19th/20th century
74.5 × 43 cm
T.169–1975
Given by Dame Joan Evans

64

66

67

68

67
Detail from a length of cotton muslin embroidered in coloured silks in satin stitch. Shades of green, mauve, pink and blue, with yellow silk scrolling to represent gold. This is professional work, the material probably intended for women's trousers (*shalwar*) – see p. 16. The design shows strong west European influence.
19th century
Spray of flowers c. 17 cm
T.111–1964
Given by HM Queen Mary

68
Part of an embroidered caftan. Tambour embroidery in coloured silks on white silk. Shades of red, mauve, blue, green and brown.
19th century
Depth of border 10 cm
Circ. 166–1920

69

Stitches. Nos. 69–73

69
Detail from a curtain (cat. 4) to show darning stitch worked on the counted threads of a linen ground.
17th century
Size of detail 10 × 7.5 cm
908–1892

70
Detail from a cover (Colour plate 7) worked in laid and couched silks on a silk satin ground. Details are worked in couched metal thread over padding stitches, which can be seen where the metal thread has worn away. The motifs are outlined with a double couched metal thread, which has also worn to the silk core in places.
17th–18th century
Size of detail 9 × 11 cm
T.733–1950
Given by Professor R. M. Dawkins

70

71

Detail from the border of a scarf
(Colour plate 13) to show a compound
double running stitch worked in silk
on fine linen. Details are worked in
couched metal thread.
? Late 17th century
Size of detail 8 × 9 cm
T.171–1975
Given by Dame Joan Evans

72

Detail from the border of a towel
worked in coloured silks and metal
thread on cotton. The open stitch
(*mürver*) is worked in four stages in
vertical and horizontal steps, pulling
the threads of the ground material
apart to create an open net. The
embroidery looks the same on both
faces.
18th–19th century
Size of detail 9.5 × 8.5 cm
2024–1876
Sandwith Collection. Acquired in
Crete

71

72

73

73
Detail from the border of a towel
(Colour plate 21) to show shaded
double running stitch worked in
coloured silks on fine linen. Typically,
several shades of each colour are used,
and the embroidery is identical on
both surfaces.
18th century
Size of detail 6.5 × 8.5 cm
Circ. 196–1931